The Effective Low-Carb Instant Pot Cookbook

Fast & Easy Low Carbohydrate Recipes to Help You Lose Weight and Start Living a Healthy Lifestyle

Chef Effect

Table of Contents

DEDICATION

This book is dedicated to everyone who wants to start living a healthy lifestyle with the help of a low-carb diet but does not have enough time to make elaborate and time-consuming dishes. This book provides healthy and delicious low-carb recipes using a highly convenient device—the Instant Pot.

INTRODUCTION

The link between lifestyle and health has long been established in *scientific research*[1].

According to a *report*[2] by the World Health Organization (WHO), up to 60 percent of factors that affect not only one's health, but also one's quality of life, are related to lifestyle.

Among the various aspects of lifestyle, dieting is confirmed to be the most significant factor that directly affects the health.

A poor diet can increase the risk of many health problems, including heart disease, obesity, diabetes and many others, reports a *study*[3] published in the *New England Journal of Medicine*.

To avoid all these problems, it's important to adopt a healthy lifestyle, starting with a nutritious and well-balanced diet.

One of the diet programs that has grown in popularity over the recent years is the low-carb diet, which is a low-carb, moderate-protein, and high-fat diet that's been proven to have numerous benefits for the health.

This book will guide you through the program, providing not only vital information about the diet, but also delicious and healthy meals that you will love.

But instead of providing complicated and time-consuming dishes, you'll be getting Instant Pot recipes that are very simple and easy to make. Have fun!

CHAPTER 1 - AN OVERVIEW

WHAT IS THE LOW-CARB DIET?

The Low-Carb diet works by prompting the body to mainly use fat for energy instead of storing it in the body tissues.

Here's how it works:

When you eat food that's rich in carbohydrates, the body produces *glucose*[4] and *insulin*[5].

- **Glucose** – Glucose is converted by the body into usable energy. It is the body's most preferred energy source.
- **Insulin** – Insulin is manufactured by the body to process the glucose.

When the body uses glucose for energy, it stores the fats inside the body. This is what causes weight gain.

Excessive weight gain, as you know, can lead to a number of ailments, such as hypertension, heart disease, diabetes and so on.

By taking on a low-carb diet, the body is forced to undergo a state called *ketosis*[6].

WHAT IS KETOSIS?

Ketosis is a process wherein the body produces *ketones*[7], which are the byproducts of fat breakdown in the liver. The ketones then become the primary source of energy, instead of carbohydrates.

By using ketones as an energy source, the body benefits in more ways than one. This results not only in weight loss but also in better physical and mental performance.

This is primarily how the low-carb diet works.

WHAT ARE THE ADVANTAGES & DISADVANTAGES?

Let's look at the major benefits of the low-carb diet:

- **Weight loss** – Since the body uses fat as its main energy source instead of carbohydrates, fat is no longer stored inside the body. This results in significant weight loss. Not only that, this diet also reduces the level of insulin, helping the body burn more fat. It also works in reducing body mass index (BMI) and body weight in obese patients.

- **Blood sugar control** – The low-carb diet has been proven to lower blood sugar levels. In fact, studies have shown that it is highly effective in preventing and managing type 2 diabetes.

  Researchers from the United States conducted a *clinical trial* [8]that proved that this diet improved glycemic control among patients with type 2 diabetes, causing a reduction in the use of diabetes medication.

  Better mental focus – It has also been found that the low-carb diet significantly boosts mental focus and performance. Why? That's because ketones are an excellent fuel for the brain. This diet has strong "neuroprotective effects" that can significantly enhance cognition, memory and behavior.

- **Increased energy** – Even though the body prefers carbohydrates, ketones are a more stable source of energy. When you start the low-carb diet, you will notice higher energy levels that are sustained throughout the day. This diet is also known to improve aerobic performance as well as exercise metabolism.

- **Epilepsy treatment** – What many people do not know is that the low-carb diet was originally formulated as treatment for epilepsy. Many studies have provided sufficient evidence that this diet works in decreasing the frequency of seizures among children and adults diagnosed with epilepsy.

- **Blood pressure and cholesterol control** – Surprisingly, even though this diet is high in fat, it helps stabilize the cholesterol and blood pressure levels, and that's because the fats used in this diet are healthy fats. This was proven in a 2013 *study* [9]published in the *American Journal of Physiology*.

It's important to know, however, that there have also been a few reports of side effects from the low-carb diet users. These include:

- Changes in bowel habits (diarrhea or constipation)
- Leg cramps
- Bad breath

It's also possible to experience flu-like symptoms, which is common among first-time users of the low-carb diet. It causes the following symptoms:

- Dizziness
- Nausea
- Fatigue

- Insomnia
- Inability to focus
- Palpitations when lying down
- Cravings

Fortunately, most of these side effects go away after a few days or weeks, once the body has adjusted to the new diet.

How Much Carb and Fat are Allowed?

Here's the diet portion to be observed when using the low-carb diet:

- 60 to 75 percent of calories from fat
- 15 to 30 percent of calories from protein
- 5 to 10 percent of calories from carbohydrates

There are other factors to consider as well, such as height, weight and body mass index.

Who Should Be on this Diet?

The low-carb diet is ideal for the following people:

- People who want to lose weight.
- People who want to start living a healthy lifestyle.
- People who are at risk of diabetes.
- People who are at risk of high blood pressure and heart disease.
- People who have epilepsy.

This diet, however, is not recommended for the following individuals:

- People who have liver, pancreatic or kidney ailments.
- People who have already been diagnosed with type 1 diabetes.
- Women who are pregnant or breastfeeding.
- People who suffer from eating disorders.

Yields: 4 servings
Serving size: 1 cup
Preparation Time: 5 minutes
Cooking Time: 30 minutes
Passive Time: 0 minutes
Total Time: 35 minutes

Ingredients

- 1 tbsp. olive oil
- 1 tbsp. garlic, minced
- ½ cup onion, diced
- 1 lb. beef stew meat
- 1 ½ cups mushrooms, chopped
- ¾ cup water
- 1 tsp. salt
- 1 tsp. pepper
- 1 tbsp. Worcestershire sauce
- ½ cup sour cream
- ¼ tsp. xanthan gum

Instructions

1. Set your Instant Pot to the sauté mode.
2. Pour in the olive oil.
3. Add the garlic and onions.
4. Cook until the garlic is golden brown and the onions are soft.
5. Add the rest of the ingredients, except the sour cream and xanthan gum.
6. Seal the lid.
7. Cook on high for 20 minutes.
8. Release the pressure naturally.
9. Open the pot and set it to the sauté mode.
10. Pour the sour cream and stir.
11. Gradually add the xanthan gum.
12. Stir until the consistency thickens.
13. Serve with low-carb noodles.

Nutritional Information per Serving

Calories 321

Total Fat 16 g

Cholesterol 98 mg

Sodium 690 mg

Potassium 599 mg

Total Carbs 9 g

Protein 33 g

Substitution/s:

Xanthan gum may be replaced with arrowroot starch or cornstarch diluted in water.

Yields: 5 servings

Serving size: 3 meatballs, ½ cup sauce

Preparation Time: 15 minutes

Cooking Time: 15 minutes

Passive Time: 0 minutes

Total Time: 30 minutes

Ingredients

- 1 ½ lb. lean ground beef
- ½ cup almond flour
- ¾ cup Parmesan cheese, grated
- 2 tbsp. parsley, chopped
- 2 eggs
- ¼ tsp. garlic powder
- 1 tsp. onion powder
- ¼ tsp. dried oregano
- 1 tsp. salt
- ¼ tsp. black pepper
- 1 tsp. olive oil
- 3 cups keto marinara sauce

Instructions

1. Combine the ground beef, flour, Parmesan cheese, parsley, eggs, garlic powder, onion powder, dried oregano, salt and black pepper in a bowl.
2. Mix well.
3. Form 15 small meatballs.
4. Pour the olive oil into the Instant Pot.
5. Turn on the sauté mode.
6. Brown all sides of the meatballs.
7. Pour the marinara sauce over the meatballs.
8. Put on the lid.
9. Set the mode to manual.
10. Select low and cook for 10 minutes.
11. Serve the meatballs with green salad or cauliflower rice.

Nutritional Information per Serving

Calories 455

Total Fat 33 g

Cholesterol 178 mg

Sodium 860 mg

Potassium 886 mg

Total Carbs 19.4 g

Protein 34 g

Substitution/s:

You may use garlic salt instead of garlic powder, and basil instead of oregano.

Balsamic Pot Roast

Yields: 10 servings

Serving size: 4 oz. pot roast

Preparation Time: 5 minutes

Cooking Time: 1 hour

Passive Time: 0 minutes

Total Time: 1 hour and 5 minutes

Ingredients

- 1 tbsp. salt
- 1 tsp. black ground pepper
- 1 tsp. garlic powder
- 3 lb. beef chuck roast (boneless)
- ½ cup onion, diced
- ¼ cup balsamic vinegar
- 2 cups water, divided
- ¼ tsp. xanthan gum
- ¼ cup fresh parsley, chopped

Instructions

1. Slice the chuck roast in half.
2. Rub the salt, pepper and garlic powder on both sides of the chuck roast.
3. Turn on the sauté setting of the Instant Pot.
4. Brown both sides of the chuck roast.
5. Add the onions, balsamic vinegar and half of the water over the meat.
6. Cover the pot.
7. Set it to manual and cook for 35 minutes.
8. Release the pressure naturally.
9. Remove the lid.
10. Transfer the meat to a bowl.
11. Break into smaller chunks.
12. Add the remaining water to the pot.
13. Simmer for 10 minutes using the sauté setting.
14. Add the xanthan gum and the meat.
15. Garnish with parsley before serving.

Nutritional Information per Serving

Calories 299

Total Fat 11.3 g
Cholesterol 137 mg
Sodium 804 mg
Potassium 418 mg
Total Carbs 1.3 g
Protein 45.1 g

Beef Lasagna

Yields: 8 servings

Serving size: 1 bowl

Preparation Time: 10 minutes

Cooking Time: 25 minutes

Passive Time: 0 minutes

Total Time: 35 minutes

Ingredients

- 1 onion, chopped
- 2 cloves garlic, crushed and minced
- 1 lb. ground beef
- 1 ½ cups ricotta cheese
- ½ cup Parmesan cheese, grated
- 1 egg
- 25 oz. keto marinara sauce
- 8 oz. mozzarella cheese, sliced
- 2 tbsp. parsley, chopped

Instructions

1. Turn the Instant Pot to the sauté setting.
2. Sauté the onions and garlic for 3 to 5 minutes.
3. Add the ground beef and cook until brown.
4. In a bowl, mix the ricotta, Parmesan cheese and the egg.
5. Add the marinara sauce into the pot.
6. Take half of the meat sauce and set aside.
7. Put half of the mozzarella cheese on top of the pot.
8. Spread half of the ricotta-Parmesan mixture on top of the mozzarella.
9. Add the remaining meat sauce you set aside earlier.
10. Add the remaining mozzarella cheese.
11. Spread the remaining ricotta-Parmesan mixture.
12. Cover the pot.
13. Cook on high for 10 minutes.
14. Release the steam.
15. Ladle the lasagna into serving bowls.
16. Sprinkle the chopped parsley on top before serving.

Nutritional Information per Serving

Calories 339

Total Fat 14.3 g

Cholesterol 108 mg

Sodium 650 mg

Potassium 315 mg

Total Carbs 7.9 g

Protein 36 g

Substitution/s:

If you don't like to use beef, you can use ground turkey or chicken.

Mississippi Pot Roast

Yields: 8 servings

Serving size: 6 oz. pot roast

Preparation Time: 5 minutes

Cooking Time: 70 minutes

Passive Time: 0 minutes

Total Time: 75 minutes

Ingredients

- 3 lb. beef chuck roast
- 16 oz. jarred pepperoncini, drained (reserve the brine)
- 1 tbsp. dried chives
- 1 tbsp. dried parsley
- 1 tbsp. onion powder
- 1 tbsp. garlic powder
- 1 tbsp. dried dill
- ½ tsp. salt
- ¼ tsp. black pepper
- ½ cup butter

Instructions

1. Put the chuck roast in your Instant Pot.
2. Add the pepperoncini on top.
3. Add 1 cup of the reserved brine.
4. Add the chives, parsley, onion powder, garlic powder, dill, salt and pepper into the pot.
5. Mix well.
6. Put the butter on top of the roast.
7. Seal the pot.
8. Cook on high for 70 minutes.
9. Release the pressure.
10. Remove the meat from the pot.
11. Shred the meat with two forks.
12. Serve with salad or low-carb soup.

Nutritional Information per Serving

Calories 435.2

Total Fat 31.64 g

Cholesterol 127 mg

Sodium 185 mg
Potassium 309 mg
Total Carbs 1.3 g
Protein 33.2 g

Beef Goulash

Yields: 8 servings

Serving size: 1 bowl

Preparation Time: 5 minutes

Cooking Time: 30 minutes

Passive Time: 0 minutes

Total Time: 35 minutes

Ingredients

- 2 lb. lean ground beef
- 3 tsp. olive oil, divided
- 1 red bell pepper, sliced into strips
- 1 onion, sliced
- 2 tbsp. sweet paprika
- ½ tsp. cayenne pepper
- 1 tbsp. garlic, minced
- 4 cups homemade beef stock
- 29 oz. canned diced tomatoes

Instructions

1. Set the setting of your Instant Pot to sauté.
2. Pour 2 teaspoons olive oil into the pot.
3. Brown the ground beef.
4. Remove from the pot and drain.
5. Add the remaining olive oil into the pot.
6. Cook the onions and peppers for 4 minutes.
7. Add the paprika, cayenne pepper and garlic.
8. Cook for 3 minutes. Stir frequently.
9. Pour the beef stock, diced tomatoes and cooked ground beef.
10. Cover the pot.
11. Set to soup setting.
12. Set the timer to 15 minutes.
13. Release the pressure manually.

Nutritional Information per Serving

Calories 310

Total Fat 11.4 g

Cholesterol 101 mg

Sodium 206 mg

Potassium 795 mg

Total Carbs 8.2 g

Protein 38.3 g

Substitution/s:

Cayenne pepper may be substituted with hot paprika.

CUBAN BEEF

Yields: 8 servings

Serving size: 1 bowl

Preparation Time: 20 minutes

Cooking Time: 50 minutes

Passive Time: 0 minutes

Total Time: 1 hour and 10 minutes

Ingredients

- Salt and pepper to taste
- 2 lb. beef flank steak
- 1 tbsp. olive oil
- 4 cloves garlic, crushed and minced
- 1 onion, chopped
- 1 cup beef stock
- 15 oz. canned diced tomatoes
- 1 bay leaf
- 1 tsp. ground cumin
- ½ tsp. dried oregano
- 2 cups sweet peppers, sliced
- ½ adobo seasoning
- ½ cup fresh parsley, chopped
- 2 tbsp. white wine vinegar
- ½ cup green olives, chopped

Instructions

1. Rub the salt and pepper into the beef flank steak.
2. Pour the olive oil into the Instant Pot.
3. Set to thesauté mode.
4. Brown both sides of the beef flank steak.
5. Transfer to a plate.
6. Add the garlic and onions.
7. Cook for 4 to 5 minutes, stirring frequently.
8. Add the beef stock.
9. Scrape the browned bits from the pot using a wooden spatula.
10. Mix in the canned tomatoes, bay leaf, cumin, oregano and sweet peppers.
11. Return the beef flank steak to the pot.
12. Mix well.

13. Seal the pot and cook on high for 40 minutes.

14. Release the pressure naturally.

15. Shred the meat with two forks.

16. Remove the bay leaf.

17. Add the parsley, green olives and vinegar.

18. Ladle the soup into a bowl.

19. Top with the shredded beef.

Nutritional Information per Serving

Calories 258

Total Fat 9.2 g

Cholesterol 101 mg

Sodium 201 mg

Potassium 711 mg

Total Carbs 6.6 g

Protein 35.6 g

Substitution/s:

You may replace the white wine vinegar with apple cider vinegar.

Korean Barbecue Beef

Yields: 12 servings

Serving size: 4 oz. barbecue beef

Preparation Time: 5 minutes

Cooking Time: 40 minutes

Passive Time: 0 minutes

Total Time: 45 minutes

Ingredients

- 5 lb. beef chuck roast (boneless)
- ½ cup water
- ¼ cup fish sauce (sugar-free)
- 2 tbsp. ginger, grated
- 3 cloves garlic, crushed
- 1 tsp. orange extract
- 2.5 tbsp. granulated sugar substitute
- 1 tsp. red pepper flakes, crushed
- 1 tbsp. orange zest
- 1 tsp. red wine vinegar
- ¼ cup sugar-free mayonnaise
- 1 tsp. hot sauce
- Lettuce leaves for garnish

Instructions

1. Place the chuck roast in the Instant Pot.
2. Add the water, fish sauce, ginger, garlic, orange extract, 2 tablespoons of sugar substitute and red pepper flakes.
3. Cover the pot.
4. Set to manual and cook on high for 35 minutes.
5. Release the pressure naturally.
6. Uncover the pot.
7. Mix in the orange zest and red wine vinegar.
8. Set to the sauté mode and cook for 5 minutes.
9. Remove the meat and shred using two forks.
10. In a bowl, mix the mayo, hot sauce and remaining teaspoon of sugar substitute.
11. Serve the beef with the spicy mayo sauce and lettuce leaves.

Nutritional Information per Serving

Calories 695
Total Fat 19.7 g
Cholesterol 195 mg
Sodium 596 mg
Potassium 235 mg
Total Carbs 1.4 g
Protein 25 g

Corned Beef with Cabbage

Yields: 12 servings

Serving size: 1 cup

Preparation Time: 15 minutes

Cooking Time: 1 hour and 15 minutes

Passive Time: 0 minutes

Total Time: 1 hour and 30 minutes

Ingredients

- 4 lb. corned beef brisket
- 6 cups water
- 4 cloves garlic, crushed
- 2 tsp. dried mustard
- 2 tsp. black peppercorns
- 2 onions, sliced
- 1 head cabbage, cut into wedges
- 4 carrots, sliced into thirds
- 1 cup celery, chopped

Instructions

1. Place the corned beef brisket in the Instant pot.
2. Add the water.
3. Add the garlic, mustard and black peppercorns.
4. Cover the pot.
5. Set the mode to stew.
6. Cook on high for 1 hour.
7. Release the pressure naturally.
8. Remove the lid carefully.
9. Transfer the beef onto a plate.
10. Add the onion, cabbage, carrots and celery.
11. Set the mode to soup.
12. Cook for 15 minutes.
13. Use the quick release method.
14. Put the beef back into the pot.
15. Mix well.
16. Serve while warm.

Nutritional Information per Serving

Calories 334

Total Fat 22.8 g
Cholesterol 81 mg
Sodium 1.8 g
Potassium 537 mg
Total Carbs 8.1 g
Protein 23.7 g

Beef Keema

Yields: 2 servings
Serving size: 1 cup
Preparation Time: 5 minutes
Cooking Time: 1 hour
Passive Time: 0 minutes
Total Time: 1 hour and 5 minutes

Ingredients

- 2 tbsp. ghee
- 1 onion, chopped
- 5 cloves garlic, crushed and minced
- 1 tbsp. ginger, minced
- 1 Serrano pepper, minced
- 1 tbsp. coriander powder
- ½ tsp. turmeric
- 1 tsp. salt
- ½ tsp. black pepper
- ½ tsp. cumin powder
- 1 tsp. paprika
- ½ tsp. garam masala
- ¼ tsp. ground cardamom
- ¼ tsp. cayenne
- 1 lb. ground beef
- 14 ½ oz. canned diced tomatoes
- 2 cups peas

Instructions

1. Place the ghee in the Instant Pot.
2. Add the onions.
3. Set to sauté and cook for 10 minutes.
4. Add the garlic, ginger, pepper, coriander, turmeric, salt, pepper, cumin, paprika, garam masala, cardamom and cayenne.
5. Mix well and cook for 1 minute.
6. Add the ground beef.
7. Cook until the ground beef is brown.
8. Add in the diced tomatoes and peas.
9. Cover the lid.

10. Press the keep warm setting.

11. After a few seconds, press the bean/chili setting.

12. Set the timer to 30 minutes.

13. Release the pressure naturally.

14. Press the sauté setting and cook for 10 minutes or until the liquid is reduced.

Nutritional Information per Serving

Calories 741

Total Fat 28.5 g

Cholesterol 235 mg

Sodium 1.3 g

Potassium 1.9 mg

Total Carbs 40.5 g

Protein 38.3 g

Chicken Tikka Masala

Yields: 4 servings

Serving size: 1 cup

Preparation Time: 10 minutes

Cooking Time: 20 minutes

Passive Time: 1 hour

Total Time: 1 hour and 30 minutes

Ingredients

- 1 lb. chicken breasts (boneless and skinless), chopped into small pieces

For the chicken marinade:

- 1 tbsp. freshly squeezed lemon juice
- 1 tbsp. garam masala
- 1 cup low-fat Greek yogurt
- ¼ tsp. ground ginger
- 1 tsp. black pepper

For the sauce:

- 5 cloves garlic, crushed and minced
- 15 oz. canned tomato puree
- 4 tsp. garam masala
- ¼ tsp. cayenne
- ½ tsp. turmeric
- ½ tsp. paprika
- ½ tsp. salt
- 1 cup heavy whipping cream

For serving:

- Lettuce leaves
- Cilantro, chopped

Instructions

1. In a bowl, combine the lemon juice, garam masala, yogurt, ginger and black pepper.
2. Add the chicken cubes into the bowl.
3. Cover with cling wrap.

4. Place in the refrigerator for 1 hour.
5. Select the sauté setting on your Instant Pot.
6. Add the chicken cubes and marinade.
7. Cook for 5 minutes, stirring frequently to cook evenly.
8. Add the garlic, tomato puree, garam masala, cayenne, turmeric, paprika and salt.
9. Cover the pot.
10. Press the manual button.
11. Cook on high for10 minutes.
12. Use quick pressure release.
13. Set the pot to sauté mode.
14. Add the cream, and mix well.
15. Simmer for 5 minutes.
16. Serve with lettuce leaves and cilantro.

Nutritional Information per Serving

Calories 460

Total Fat 27 g

Cholesterol 171 mg

Sodium 970 mg

Potassium 320 mg

Total Carbs 19 g

Protein 32 g

Substitution/s:

If tomato puree is not available, you can also use tomato sauce.

Creamy Chicken Soup

Yields: 8 servings

Serving size: 1 bowl

Preparation Time: 10 minutes

Cooking Time: 40 minutes

Passive Time: 3 hours

Total Time: 3 hours and 50 minutes

Ingredients

- 6 chicken thighs (boneless), sliced into cubes
- 4 tbsp. butter
- 8 oz. cream cheese
- 1 tsp. dried thyme
- ½ cup onion, chopped
- 4 tsp. garlic, minced
- ¼ cup celery, chopped
- 6 oz. mushrooms, sliced
- Salt and pepper to taste
- 3 cups reduced-sodium chicken stock
- 2 cups fresh spinach
- 1 cup heavy cream
- 1 lb. bacon, cooked and chopped

Instructions

1. Put the chicken cubes in a Ziplock bag.
2. Add the butter, cream cheese, thyme, onion, garlic, celery, mushrooms, salt and pepper.
3. Seal the bag.
4. Let sit in the refrigerator for 3 hours.
5. Pour the chicken mixture into your Instant Pot.
6. Add the chicken stock.
7. Press the soup setting.
8. Cook for 30 minutes.
9. Add the spinach and cream.
10. Cover and simmer for 10 minutes.
11. Sprinkle chopped bacon on top before serving.

Nutritional Information per Serving

Calories 584

Total Fat 22.5 g

Cholesterol 181 mg

Sodium 1.4 g

Potassium 614 mg

Total Carbs 3.4 g

Protein 25.3 g

Substitution/s:

You can also top the soup with chopped onion chives instead of bacon.

CHICKEN & LENTILS

Yields: 8 servings

Serving size: 1 1/3 cup

Preparation Time: 10 minutes

Cooking Time: 30 minutes

Passive Time: 0 minutes

Total Time: 40 minutes

Ingredients

- 12 oz. chicken thighs (boneless and skinless), cut into small pieces
- 1 lb. dried lentils
- 1 onion, chopped
- 3 cloves garlic, crushed and minced
- 1 tomato, diced
- ¼ cup cilantro, chopped
- 2 scallions, chopped
- 7 cups low-sodium chicken stock
- ½ tsp. paprika
- 1 tsp. cumin
- ¼ tsp. oregano
- 1 tsp. garlic powder
- Salt to taste

Instructions

1. Put all the ingredients in your Instant Pot.
2. Mix well.
3. Set the pot to the soup setting.
4. Cook for 30 minutes.
5. Release the pressure manually.
6. Serve warm.

Nutritional Information per Serving

Calories 129

Total Fat 20.5 g

Cholesterol 36 mg

Sodium 496 mg

Potassium 285 mg

Total Carbs 16 g

Protein 15 g

Substitution/s:
You can substitute the tomato with 1 cup of tomato sauce.

Creamy Salsa Chicken

Yields: 6 servings

Serving size: 1 cup

Preparation Time: 10 minutes

Cooking Time: 20 minutes

Passive Time: 0 minutes

Total Time: 30 minutes

Ingredients

- 2 ½ lb. chicken breasts
- ½ cup reduced-sodium chicken stock
- ½ cup cottage cheese
- 4 oz. cream cheese
- 1 cup salsa
- ¼ cup sour cream
- 1 tsp. taco seasoning
- ¼ cup avocado, chopped
- ¼ cup black beans
- ¼ cup cheddar cheese, shredded

Instructions

1. Add the chicken breasts to the Instant Pot.
2. Pour the chicken stock over the chicken breasts.
3. Set to poultry mode.
4. Put on the lid.
5. Cook for 10 minutes.
6. Use the quick pressure release.
7. Transfer the chicken to a plate.
8. Shred using 2 forks.
9. Reserve a ½ cup of the chicken stock from the pot.
10. Discard the remaining liquid.
11. Add the cottage cheese, cream cheese, salsa, sour cream and taco seasoning to the pot.
12. Pour the reserved stock back into the pot.
13. Set to the sauté mode.
14. Cook for 10 minutes.
15. Put the shredded chicken back into the pot.
16. Mix well.
17. Serve with avocado, black beans and cheddar cheese.

Nutritional Information per Serving

Calories 529

Total Fat 23.9 g

Cholesterol 224 mg

Sodium 651 mg

Potassium 796 mg

Total Carbs 4 g

Protein 50.7 g

Substitution/s:

You can use fajita seasoning instead of taco seasoning.

Yields: 6 servings

Serving size: 1 to 2 pieces of chicken

Preparation Time: 5 minutes

Cooking Time: 35 minutes

Passive Time: 5 minutes

Total Time: 45 minutes

Ingredients

- 1 whole chicken, cavity parts removed
- 1 lemon, sliced in half
- 1 onion, cut into quarters
- 1 tsp. paprika
- 1 tsp. granulated garlic
- Salt and pepper to taste
- 2 tbsp. avocado oil
- 1 cup chicken broth

Instructions

1. Rinse the whole chicken.
2. Pat it dry using a paper towel.
3. Insert the lemon and onion into the chicken's cavity.
4. On a small plate, combine the paprika, granulated garlic, salt and pepper.
5. Set the Instant Pot to the sauté mode to preheat.
6. Rub the chicken with avocado oil and the spice mixture.
7. Put the chicken inside the Instant Pot.
8. Cook for 5 minutes.
9. Flip the chicken onto the other side.
10. Cook for 5 more minutes.
11. Add the chicken broth.
12. Cover the pot.
13. Press the manual setting.
14. Cook on high for 25 minutes.
15. Release the pressure naturally.
16. Uncover the pot.
17. Transfer the chicken to a serving platter.
18. Let it rest for 5 minutes before slicing.

Nutritional Information per Serving

Calories 640

Total Fat 25 g

Cholesterol 289 mg

Sodium 408 mg

Potassium 879 mg

Total Carbs 2.7 g

Protein 35.2 g

Substitution/s:

If avocado oil is not available, you may use coconut oil or any other oil with a high smoke point.

Chicken Stew

Yields: 8 servings

Serving size: 1 piece of chicken, ¼ cup sauce

Preparation Time: 5 minutes

Cooking Time: 30 minutes

Passive Time: 4 hours

Total Time: 4 hours and 35 minutes

Ingredients

- 3 tbsp. Worcestershire sauce
- ½ tsp. ground black pepper
- 2 tbsp. white vinegar
- 2 tbsp. achiote paste
- 1 tsp. dried oregano
- 1 tsp. ground cumin
- 1 tbsp. granulated sugar substitute
- 4 chicken thighs
- 4 chicken drumsticks
- 1 tbsp. coconut oil
- 3 cloves garlic, sliced
- 1 cup yellow onion, sliced
- 2 cups low-sodium chicken stock
- Cilantro, chopped

Instructions

1. In a bowl, mix the Worcestershire sauce, black pepper, vinegar, achiote paste, oregano, cumin and sugar substitute. Mix well.
2. Reserve 1/3 of the mixture.
3. Soak the chicken in the remaining marinade for 4 hours.
4. Place an insert into the Instant Pot.
5. Set to sauté mode.
6. Pour the coconut oil.
7. Add the chicken and cook until brown on both sides.
8. Transfer the chicken to a plate.
9. Add the garlic and onions into the pot.
10. Sauté for 3 minutes.
11. Put the chicken back into the pot.
12. Pour in the chicken stock and the reserved marinade.

13. Mix well.
14. Cover the pot.
15. Set it to manual.
16. Cook on high for 20 minutes.
17. Release the pressure naturally.
18. Garnish with cilantro before serving.

Nutritional Information per Serving

Calories 212

Total Fat 8.5 g

Cholesterol 85 mg

Sodium 162 mg

Potassium 261 mg

Total Carbs 3.4 g

Protein 28.3 g

Yields: 8 servings

Serving size: 1 piece of chicken, 1 cup sauce

Preparation Time: 5 minutes

Cooking Time: 30 minutes

Passive Time: 3 hours

Total Time: 3 hours and 35 minutes

Ingredients

- 4 lb. chicken legs and thighs

For the marinade:

- 2 tbsp. olive oil
- 1 tbsp. curry powder
- 1 tsp. onion powder
- 1 tsp. garlic powder
- 1 tsp. salt

For the curry:

- 1 tbsp. curry powder
- 1 cup water
- 2 cups coconut milk
- 4 cups cauliflower florets
- 1 tbsp. granulated sugar substitute

For garnish:

- ¼ cup cilantro, chopped

Instructions

1. Make the marinade by mixing the olive oil, curry powder, onion powder, garlic powder and salt in a bowl.
2. Soak the chicken in the marinade.
3. Cover the bowl and refrigerate for 3 hours.
4. Set the Instant Pot to the sauté mode.
5. Brown the chicken on both sides.
6. Add the curry powder, water, coconut milk, cauliflower florets and sugar substitute to the pot.
7. Cover the pot.

8. Set it to manual.
9. Cook on high for 25 minutes.
10. Use the natural pressure release mode.
11. Garnish with the cilantro before serving.

Nutritional Information per Serving

Calories 414

Total Fat 29 g

Cholesterol 71 mg

Sodium 363 mg

Potassium 597 mg

Total Carbs 8.5 g

Protein 30 g

Zuppa Toscana

Yields: 6 servings

Serving size: 1 bowl

Preparation Time: 5 minutes

Cooking Time: 20 minutes

Passive Time: 0 minute

Total Time: 25 minutes

Ingredients

- 2 tbsp. olive oil
- 1 yellow onion, chopped
- 3 cloves garlic, crushed and minced
- 1 lb. chicken sausage
- 5 cups chicken stock
- 1 tsp. dried fennel
- 2 tsp. dried basil
- 2 cups fresh kale, chopped
- ½ cup coconut milk
- Salt and pepper to taste
- 1 tbsp. red pepper, crushed

Instructions

1. Set the Instant Pot to sauté mode.
2. Pour the olive oil into the pot.
3. Sauté the onions for 3 minutes.
4. Add the garlic and chicken sausage.
5. Cook for 5 minutes.
6. Press the cancel button.
7. Pour the chicken stock over the sausage, onions and garlic.
8. Season with the dried fennel and dried basil.
9. Mix well.
10. Cover the pot.
11. Set to manual.
12. Cook on high for 12 minutes.
13. Use the quick pressure release.
14. Uncover the pot.
15. Press the sauté function.
16. Mix in the kale and coconut milk.

17. Season with the salt, pepper and red pepper.

Nutritional Information per Serving

Calories 184

Total Fat 13.7 g

Cholesterol 75 mg

Sodium 784 mg

Potassium 247 mg

Total Carbs 10 g

Protein 6.5 g

Substitution/s:

You can replace the coconut milk with heavy cream.

Chicken Vindaloo

Yields: 4 servings

Serving size: 1 piece of chicken, ¼ cup sauce

Preparation Time: 15 minutes

Cooking Time: 35 minutes

Passive Time: 4 hours

Total Time: 4 hours and 50 minutes

Ingredients

- Cooking spray
- 1 cup onion, diced
- 5 cloves garlic, crushed and minced
- 1 tbsp. ginger, grated
- ¼ cup white vinegar
- 1 cup tomato, chopped
- 1 tsp. salt
- 1 tsp. garam masala
- 1 tsp. smoked paprika
- ½ tsp. ground coriander
- ½ tsp. cayenne pepper
- ½ tsp. ground cumin
- ½ tsp. turmeric
- 1 lb. chicken thighs (boneless, skinless)
- ¼ cup water

Instructions

1. Spray cooking oil onto a cooking pan.
2. Put the pan over medium heat.
3. Cook the onions, garlic and ginger for 5 minutes.
4. In a blender, place the sautéed onions, garlic and ginger.
5. Add the white vinegar, tomatoes, salt, garam masala, paprika, coriander, cayenne pepper and cumin.
6. Pulse until smooth.
7. Add the turmeric.
8. Mix well.
9. Soak the chicken in the marinade for 4 hours.
10. Add the chicken with the marinade into the Instant Pot.
11. Set to manual mode.

12. Cook on high for 15 minutes.

13. Release the pressure naturally.

14. Press the sauté function and cook for 15 more minutes.

Nutritional Information per Serving

Calories 199

Total Fat 22 g

Cholesterol 101 mg

Sodium 686 mg

Potassium 498 mg

Total Carbs 7.5 g

Protein 23 g

Chicken with Gravy

Yields: 12 servings

Serving size: 1 to 2 pieces of chicken, 2 tbsp. gravy

Preparation Time: 5 minutes

Cooking Time: 40 minutes

Passive Time: 0 minutes

Total Time: 45 minutes

Ingredients

- 2 tbsp. olive oil, divided
- 6.5 lb. whole chicken
- ½ tsp. salt
- ½ tsp. pepper
- ½ tsp. garlic powder
- ½ tsp. onion powder
- 1 tsp. dried Italian seasoning
- 1 ½ cups reduced-sodium chicken broth
- 2 tsp. guar gum

Instructions

1. Rub half of the olive oil all over the whole chicken.
2. Pour the remaining olive oil into the Instant Pot.
3. Mix the salt, pepper, garlic powder, onion powder, and Italian seasoning in a bowl.
4. Sprinkle this mixture all over the chicken.
5. Select the sauté function to heat the oil in the pot.
6. Place the chicken with the breast side down.
7. Cook for 5 minutes.
8. Flip the chicken and cook for another 5 minutes.
9. Add the chicken broth.
10. Seal the pot.
11. Set to manual and cook on high for 40 minutes.
12. Manually release the pressure.
13. Remove the chicken from the pot.
14. Add the guar gum into the hot broth inside the pot.
15. Set to the sauté mode.
16. Stir until the gravy thickens.
17. Serve the chicken with the gravy.

Nutritional Information per Serving

Calories 450
Total Fat 20.2 g
Cholesterol 164 mg
Sodium 245 mg
Potassium 880 mg
Total Carbs 0.7 g
Protein 34.5 g

SPARE RIBS

Yields: 2 servings

Serving size: ½ lb. pork spare ribs, 1/8 cup sauce

Preparation Time: 5 minutes

Cooking Time: 20 minutes

Passive Time: 0 minutes

Total Time: 25 minutes

Ingredients

- 1 cup water
- 1 packet onion soup mix
- 1 lb. pork spare ribs
- 1 bottle buffalo sauce

Instructions

1. Place the steam rack inside the Instant Pot.
2. Add water to the bottom part of the pot.
3. Rub onion soup mix all over the spare ribs.
4. Place the ribs on top of the rack.
5. Pour the buffalo sauce over the ribs, reserving ¼ cup for serving.
6. Set to manual and cook on high for 20 minutes.
7. Release the pressure naturally.
8. Serve the spare ribs with the remaining buffalo sauce.

Nutritional Information per Serving

Calories 488

Total Fat 28.4 g

Cholesterol 111 mg

Sodium 463 mg

Potassium 26 mg

Total Carbs 10 g

Protein 40.8 g

Pork Chops with Butter Ranch Sauce

Yields: 3 servings

Serving size: 1 pork chop, 2 tbsp. sauce

Preparation Time: 5 minutes

Cooking Time: 15 minutes

Passive Time: 0 minutes

Total Time: 20 minutes

Ingredients

- ½ tbsp. coconut oil
- 3 pork chops
- ½ stick butter, sliced into cubes
- ½ packet ranch mix
- ½ cup chicken stock

Instructions

1. Pour the coconut oil into the Instant Pot.
2. Press the sauté function to heat the oil.
3. Place the pork chops inside the pot.
4. Cook until brown on both sides.
5. Put the butter cubes on top of the pork chops.
6. Sprinkle the ranch seasoning on top of the pork chops.
7. Pour the chicken stock into the pot.
8. Cover the pot.
9. Press the manual button.
10. Set the timer to 5 minutes.
11. Cook on high.
12. Let the pressure release naturally.
13. Drizzle the sauce over the pork chops before serving.

Nutritional Information per Serving

Calories 413

Total Fat 37.5 g

Cholesterol 109 mg

Sodium 314 mg

Potassium 283 mg

Total Carbs 1 g

Protein 18.3 g

Substitution/s:
You can also use avocado oil or olive oil instead of coconut oil.

Jamaican Jerk Pork Roast

Yields: 12 servings

Serving size: 4 oz. pork roast

Preparation Time: 5 minutes

Cooking Time: 1 hour

Passive Time: 0 minutes

Total Time: 1 hour and 5 minutes

Ingredients

- 1 tbsp. olive oil
- 4 lb. pork shoulder
- ¼ cup sugar-free and low-sodium Jamaican Jerk spice blend
- ½ cup low-sodium beef broth

Instructions

1. Pour the olive oil all over the pork shoulder.
2. Sprinkle the pork shoulder with the Jamaican Jerk spice blend.
3. Press the sauté setting.
4. Cook the meat until brown on all sides.
5. Pour the beef broth into the pot.
6. Cover the pot.
7. Set to manual.
8. Cook on high for 45 minutes.
9. Release the pressure.
10. Shred the pork with 2 forks.
11. Drizzle the pork with the sauce before serving.

Nutritional Information per Serving

Calories 282

Total Fat 33.6 g

Cholesterol 20 mg

Sodium 135 mg

Potassium 506 mg

Total Carbs 3 g

Protein 25.4 g

Yields: 4 servings

Serving size: 1 pork chop, 1 tbsp. sauce

Preparation Time: 5 minutes

Cooking Time: 40 minutes

Passive Time: 0 minutes

Total Time: 45 minutes

Ingredients

- 4 pork loin chops (boneless)
- 1 tsp. onion powder
- 1 tsp. garlic powder
- 1 tsp. salt
- 1 tsp. black pepper
- ¼ tsp. cayenne pepper
- 1 tbsp. paprika
- 2 tbsp. coconut oil
- ½ onion, sliced
- 6 oz. mushrooms, sliced
- 1 tbsp. butter
- ½ cup heavy cream
- ¼ tsp. xanthan gum
- 1 tbsp. fresh parsley, chopped

Instructions

1. Wash the pork chops.
2. Pat dry with paper towels.
3. In a bowl, mix the onion powder, garlic powder, salt, pepper, cayenne and paprika.
4. Rub both sides of the pork chops with 1 tablespoon of this mixture.
5. Reserve the remaining spice mixture.
6. Pour the coconut oil into the Instant Pot.
7. Press the sauté setting to heat the oil.
8. Add the pork chops.
9. Cook until brown on both sides.
10. Transfer the pork chops to a plate.
11. Add the onions and mushrooms into the pot.
12. Sauté for 2 minutes, stirring frequently.
13. Put the pork chops back into the pot.

14. Cover the pot.
15. Select the manual setting.
16. Cook on high for 25 minutes.
17. Release pressure naturally.
18. Press the sauté setting again.
19. Mix in the remaining spice mixture.
20. Add the butter, heavy cream and xanthan gum.
21. Simmer for 5 minutes.
22. Garnish with parsley before serving.

Nutritional Information per Serving

Calories 481

Total Fat 32.6 g

Cholesterol 97 mg

Sodium 880 mg

Potassium 511 mg

Total Carbs 11.8 g

Protein 14.75 g

Substitution/s:

You may also use pork cutlets for this recipe.

Sweet Pork Ribs

Yields: 6 servings

Serving size: 3 ribs, 1 tbsp. sauce

Preparation Time: 5 minutes

Cooking Time: 35 minutes

Passive Time: 0 minutes

Total Time: 40 minutes

Ingredients

- 5 lb. pork ribs, cut into sections

For the dry rub:

- 1½ tbsp. salt
- ½ tsp. ground black pepper
- 1 tsp. onion powder
- 1 tsp. garlic powder
- 1 tbsp. granulated sugar substitute
- ½ tsp. allspice
- 1 tsp. paprika
- ½ tsp. ground coriander

For the sauce:

- ½ cup sugar-free ketchup
- 2 tbsp. granulated sugar substitute
- ½ tsp. onion powder
- ½ cup water
- 2 tbsp. red wine vinegar
- ½ tbsp. ground mustard
- ½ tbsp. ground allspice
- ¼ tsp. liquid smoke

Instructions

1. Mix the salt, black pepper, onion powder, garlic powder, sugar substitute, allspice, paprika and coriander in a bowl.
2. Season all sides of the pork ribs with this mixture.
3. Place the ribs in the Instant Pot.
4. Combine the sauce ingredients.
5. Add the sauce into the pot.

6. Cover the pot and set to manual.
7. Cook on high for 35 minutes.
8. Release the pressure naturally.
9. Transfer to a serving platter, drizzle the sauce on top, and serve.

Nutritional Information per Serving

Calories 387

Total Fat 29 g

Cholesterol 146 mg

Sodium 738 mg

Potassium 420 mg

Total Carbs 0.6 g

Protein 27 g

Substitution/s:

You may use tomato puree or tomato sauce in place of ketchup.

Mexican Pork Carnitas

Yields: 11 servings

Serving size: ½ cup

Preparation Time: 5 minutes

Cooking Time: 1 hour

Passive Time: 0 minutes

Total Time: 1 hour and 5 minutes

Ingredients

- Salt and pepper to taste
- 2 ½ lb. pork shoulder blade roast (boneless)
- 6 cloves garlic, cut into slivers
- ½ tsp. sazon
- ½ tsp. garlic powder
- 1 ½ tsp. cumin
- ¼ tsp. dry adobo seasoning
- ¼ tsp. dried oregano
- ¾ cup low-sodium chicken stock
- 2 chipotle peppers in adobo sauce
- 2 bay leaves

Instructions

1. Rub the salt and pepper all over the pork.
2. In a skillet over medium-high heat, brown the pork shoulder on all sides.
3. Remove from the stove and let cool.
4. Make deep slices all over the pork shoulder.
5. Insert the garlic slivers.
6. In a bowl, mix the sazon, garlic powder, cumin, adobo seasoning and dried oregano.
7. Sprinkle this mixture all over the pork shoulder.
8. Pour the chicken stock into the Instant Pot.
9. Add the pork shoulder, chipotle peppers and bay leaves. Stir well.
10. Set to manual.
11. Cook on high for 50 minutes.
12. Release the pressure naturally.
13. Take the pork out of the pot.
14. Shred with 2 forks.
15. Serve the shredded meat with the sauce and peppers from the pot.

Nutritional Information per Serving

Calories 160
Total Fat 17 g
Cholesterol 69 mg
Sodium 397 mg
Potassium 434 mg
Total Carbs 1 g
Protein 20 g

SAUSAGES & PEPPERS

Yields: 8 servings

Serving size: 1 cup

Preparation Time: 10 minutes

Cooking Time: 30 minutes

Passive Time: 0 minutes

Total Time: 40 minutes

Ingredients

- 2 tbsp. extra virgin olive oil
- 2 lb. pork sausage, sliced
- 1 onion, chopped
- 4 cloves garlic, crushed and minced
- 2 sweet bell peppers, chopped
- 28 oz. canned diced tomatoes with juice
- 2 cups low-sodium chicken stock
- 2 tbsp. red wine vinegar
- 2 cups water
- 1 tsp. dried basil
- 1 tsp. dried parsley
- 4 oz. fresh spinach leaves, chopped
- ½ cup Parmesan cheese, grated

Instructions

1. Set the Instant Pot to the sauté mode.
2. Add the olive oil.
3. Brown the sausages for 5 minutes.
4. Remove the sausages.
5. Add the onions, garlic and sweet bell peppers.
6. Cook for 5 minutes.
7. Add the tomatoes with their juice, the broth, the vinegar and water.
8. Return the sausage to the pot.
9. Add the basil and parsley.
10. Seal the pot.
11. Set to the soup function.
12. Cook for 10 minutes.
13. Use the quick pressure release.
14. Serve with the spinach and cheese.

Nutritional Information per Serving

Calories 249

Total Fat 22.8 g

Cholesterol 91 mg

Sodium 751 mg

Potassium 420 mg

Total Carbs 1.1 g

Protein 19 g

Substitution/s:

Vegetable stock may be used in place of chicken stock.

Spanish Rice with Pork

Yields: 4 servings

Serving size: 1 cup

Preparation Time: 5 minutes

Cooking Time: 13 minutes

Passive Time: 0 minutes

Total Time: 18 minutes

Ingredients

- 1 tbsp. olive oil
- ½ onion, chopped
- 1 tbsp. garlic, crushed and minced
- 1 jalapeño, chopped
- 2 tbsp. cilantro, chopped
- ½ tsp. salt
- ½ tsp. paprika
- ½ tsp. cumin
- ½ tsp. chili powder
- 4 pork cutlets, cut into small cubes
- ½ cup low-sodium chicken stock
- 4 cups cauliflower florets
- 2 tbsp. tomato paste

Instructions

1. Press the sauté function on your Instant Pot.
2. Pour the olive oil into the pot.
3. Sauté the onions, garlic, jalapeños and cilantro for 3 minutes.
4. Add the salt, paprika, cumin and chili powder.
5. Add the pork. Mix well.
6. Pour the chicken stock into the pot.
7. Seal the pot.
8. Cook on high for 9 minutes.
9. Use the quick pressure release.
10. Uncover the pot.
11. Put the steaming basket over the chicken.
12. Place the cauliflower florets in the basket.
13. Cover the pot.
14. Cook on high for 1 minute.

15. Use the quick pressure release.
16. Break the cauliflower into rice-like pieces.
17. Mix in the tomato paste to give the rice a bright red color.
18. Serve the pork cubes and veggies with the cauliflower rice.

Nutritional Information per Serving

Calories 320

Total Fat 21.1 g

Cholesterol 95 mg

Sodium 514 mg

Potassium 467 mg

Total Carbs 9.6 g

Protein 23.5 g

Cowboy Chili

Yields: 10 servings

Serving size: 1 bowl

Preparation Time: 10 minutes

Cooking Time: 1 hour

Passive Time: 0 minutes

Total Time: 1 hour and 10 minutes

Ingredients

- 1 tbsp. olive oil
- 2 onions, diced
- 11 lb. breakfast sausage, sliced
- 1 lb. ground pork
- 1 ½ cups carrots, diced
- 29 oz. tomatoes, diced
- 1 tsp. salt
- ½ tsp. pepper
- 1 tsp. onion powder
- 1 tsp. garlic powder
- 2 tbsp. chili powder
- ½ tsp. smoked paprika
- 1 tbsp. Worcestershire sauce

Instructions

1. Press the sauté mode on your Instant Pot.
2. Sauté the onion for 3 minutes.
3. Brown the sausage and ground pork for 5 minutes.
4. Add the carrots, tomatoes, salt, pepper, onion powder, garlic powder, chili powder, paprika and Worcestershire sauce.
5. Cover the pot.
6. Set to manual.
7. Cook on high for 30 minutes.
8. Release the pressure naturally.
9. Press the bean/chili mode.
10. Cook for 10 minutes.
11. Use the quick release method.
12. Set to sauté mode.
13. Let cook for 10 more minutes.

Nutritional Information per Serving

Calories 602

Total Fat 48.3 g

Cholesterol 151 mg

Sodium 1.3 g

Potassium 659 mg

Total Carbs 2.8 g

Protein 36.8 g

Substitution/s:

You can also use ground beef or ground turkey instead of ground pork.

GREEK PORK TACOS

Yields: 8 servings

Serving size: 2 tacos

Preparation Time: 15 minutes

Cooking Time: 1 hour and 5 minutes

Passive Time: 0 minutes

Total Time: 1 hour and 20 minutes

Ingredients

- 3 tbsp. olive oil, divided
- 2 lb. pork sirloin, sliced into strips
- 1 tbsp. lemon juice
- 1 tsp. lemon zest
- ½ cup chicken stock
- ½ tsp. Greek oregano
- 1 tbsp. salt-free Greek seasoning
- Black pepper to taste
- 1 cup lettuce leaves, chopped
- 1 cup salsa
- 8 low-carb whole wheat tortillas

Instructions

1. Press the sauté function on your Instant Pot.
2. Pour 1 tablespoon of olive oil into the pot.
3. Brown the pork strips.
4. Add the lemon juice and zest, chicken stock, Greek oregano, Greek seasoning and black pepper.
5. Mix well.
6. Seal the pot.
7. Set to manual.
8. Cook on high pressure for 50 minutes.
9. Use the natural pressure release.
10. Uncover the pot.
11. Remove the pork.
12. Press the sauté function.
13. Simmer the sauce until it has thickened.
14. Heat the whole wheat tortillas in the microwave.
15. Assemble the tacos by stuffing them with the pork strips, lettuce and salsa.

16. Drizzle sauce on top before serving.

Nutritional Information per Serving

Calories 269

Total Fat 9.9 g

Cholesterol 49 mg

Sodium 403 mg

Potassium 312 mg

Total Carbs 24.5 g

Protein 21.2 g

Shrimp with Coconut Milk

Yields: 4 servings

Serving size: 6 to 7 pieces of shrimp, ½ cup sauce

Preparation Time: 10 minutes

Cooking Time: 4 minutes

Passive Time: 0 minutes

Total Time: 14 minutes

Ingredients

- 2 cups water
- 1 lb. shrimp, shelled and deveined
- 1 tbsp. garlic, minced
- 1 tbsp. ginger, minced
- 1 cup canned coconut milk (unsweetened)
- ½ tsp. turmeric
- ½ tsp. cayenne pepper
- 1 tsp. salt
- 1 tsp. garam masala

Instructions

1. Pour the water into the Instant Pot.
2. Place a trivet inside.
3. Put the shrimp and the rest of the ingredients in a smaller pot that's small enough to fit inside the Instant Pot.
4. Cover the smaller pot with foil.
5. Cook on low for 4 minutes.
6. Release the pressure quickly.
7. Serve while warm.

Nutritional Information per Serving

Calories 192

Total Fat 12 g

Cholesterol 239 mg

Sodium 868 mg

Potassium 311 mg

Total Carbs 4 g

Protein 16 g

Substitution/s:
Hot paprika may be used in place of cayenne pepper.

Steamed Fish with Ginger & Scallions

Yields: 4 servings

Serving size: 4 to 6 strips of fish

Preparation Time: 10 minutes

Cooking Time: 34 minutes

Passive Time: 30 minutes

Total Time: 1 hour and 14 minutes

Ingredients

- 2 tbsp. rice wine
- 3 tbsp. soy sauce
- 1 tbsp. black bean paste
- 1 tsp. garlic, minced
- 1 tsp. ginger, minced
- 1 lb. firm white fish fillet, sliced into strips
- 2 cups water
- 1 tbsp. peanut oil
- 2 tbsp. ginger, julienned
- ¼ cup scallions, julienned
- ¼ cup cilantro, chopped

Instructions

1. Combine the rice wine, soy sauce, black bean paste, garlic and ginger in a bowl.
2. Coat the fish strips with half of this mixture. Reserve the remaining.
3. Cover the bowl with foil.
4. Place in the refrigerator for 30 minutes.
5. Pour the water into the Instant Pot.
6. Place a steamer inside the pot.
7. Place the fish on top of the steamer.
8. Set to manual.
9. Cook on low for 2 minutes.
10. Use the quick pressure release.
11. In a pan over medium heat, add the oil, ginger, scallions, and cilantro.
12. Sauté for 2 minutes.
13. Add the reserved marinade.
14. Pour the sauce over the steamed fish before serving.

Nutritional Information per Serving

Calories 249
Total Fat 12 g
Cholesterol 87 mg
Sodium 820 mg
Potassium 519 mg
Total Carbs 5.5 g
Protein 28.7 g

Shrimp with Feta & Tomatoes

Yields: 6 servings

Serving size: 1 cup

Preparation Time: 5 minutes

Cooking Time: 12 minutes

Passive Time: 0 minutes

Total Time: 17 minutes

Ingredients

- 2 tbsp. butter
- 1 tbsp. garlic
- ½ tsp. red pepper flakes
- 1 ½ cups onion, chopped
- 1 tsp. oregano
- 1 tsp. salt
- 14 ½ oz. canned tomatoes
- 1 lb. frozen shrimp
- 1 cup feta cheese, crumbled
- ¼ cup parsley
- ½ cup black olives, sliced

Instructions

1. Set your Instant Pot to the sauté mode.
2. Add the butter.
3. Wait for it to melt a little before adding the garlic and red pepper flakes.
4. Add the onions, oregano, salt, and tomatoes.
5. Stir in the shrimp.
6. Cook for 10 minutes, stirring frequently.
7. Press the manual button.
8. Cook on low for 2 minutes.
9. Release the pressure quickly.
10. Top with the feta cheese, parsley and black olives before serving.

Nutritional Information per Serving

Calories 211

Total Fat 11 g

Cholesterol 222 mg

Sodium 1.5 g

Potassium 148 mg
Total Carbs 6 g
Protein 19 g

Seafood Congee

Yields: 4 servings

Serving size: 1 bowl

Preparation Time: 15 minutes

Cooking Time: 35 minutes

Passive Time: 0 minutes

Total Time: 50 minutes

Ingredients

- 6 cups of water
- 1 ½ oz. dried scallops
- 2 dried Shiitake mushrooms, soaked in water and chopped
- 8 oz. crab meat
- 2 cloves garlic, minced
- 1 cabbage leaf, chopped
- 1 tsp. sesame oil
- ¼ tsp. fish sauce
- 1 tsp. soy sauce
- 7 oz. scallops, sliced into quarters
- 7 frozen oysters
- 1 head cauliflower, grated to rice consistency
- 7 oz. bean curd, sliced into cubes
- Salt and pepper to taste
- 1 tbsp. spring onions, chopped

Instructions

1. Pour the water into the Instant Pot.
2. Add the dried scallops.
3. Set to manual.
4. Cook on high for 20 minutes.
5. While waiting, make the meatballs by combing the mushrooms, crab meat, garlic, cabbage leaf, sesame oil, fish sauce and soy sauce.
6. Form small meatballs from this meat mixture.
7. Release the pressure from the pot using the quick method.
8. Shred the scallops.
9. Set to the sauté mode.
10. Add in the bean curd, meatballs and scallops.
11. Cook for 15 minutes.

12. Season with salt and pepper.

13. Top with the spring onions before serving.

Nutritional Information per Serving

Calories 224

Total Fat 19.6 g

Cholesterol 71 mg

Sodium 446 mg

Potassium 860 mg

Total Carbs 14.2 g

Protein 14.9 g

Substitution/s:

Soft tofu may be used in place of bean curd.

Rosemary Salmon

Yields: 2 servings

Serving size: ½ lb. salmon, 1 cup vegetables

Preparation Time: 10 minutes

Cooking Time: 7 minutes

Passive Time: 0 minutes

Total Time: 17 minutes

Ingredients

- 1 cup water
- 1 lb. wild salmon
- 10 oz. fresh asparagus
- 1 sprig fresh rosemary
- ½ cup cherry tomatoes, sliced in half
- 1 tbsp. olive oil
- 2 tsp. lemon juice
- Salt and pepper to taste

Instructions

1. Pour the water into the Instant Pot.
2. Put a wire rack inside the pot.
3. Place the salmon on the wire rack.
4. Top it with the rosemary and asparagus.
5. Set it to manual mode.
6. Cook on high for 7 minutes.
7. Release the pressure naturally.
8. Transfer the salmon to a serving platter.
9. Discard the rosemary sprig.
10. Put the tomatoes on top of the salmon, along with the asparagus.
11. Drizzle with the olive oil and lemon juice.
12. Season with the salt and pepper.

Nutritional Information per Serving

Calories 269

Total Fat 24.4 g

Cholesterol 67 mg

Sodium 74 mg

Potassium 858 mg

Total Carbs 5.6 g
Protein 21.8 g

SEAFOOD STEW

Yields: 4 servings

Serving size: 1 bowl

Preparation Time: 10 minutes

Cooking Time: 37 minutes

Passive Time: 0 minutes

Total Time: 47 minutes

Ingredients

- 6 tbsp. olive oil
- 1 onion, chopped
- 3 cloves garlic, crushed and minced
- ¼ cup fresh parsley, chopped
- 1 ½ cups tomatoes, chopped
- 2 tsp. tomato paste
- ½ cup dry white wine
- 8 oz. clam juice
- 1 ½ lb. halibut fillet, sliced into small pieces.
- ½ lb. shrimp, peeled and deveined
- ¼ tsp. dried oregano
- ¼ tsp. dried thyme
- ¼ tsp. Tabasco hot sauce
- Salt and pepper to taste

Instructions

1. Set the Instant Pot to sauté.
2. Pour the olive oil into the pot.
3. Add the onions and garlic.
4. Sauté for 5 minutes.
5. Add the parsley and cook for 2 minutes, stirring frequently.
6. Add in the tomatoes and tomato paste.
7. Let cook for10 minutes.
8. Add the dry white wine, clam juice, fish and shrimp.
9. Cover with the lid.
10. Turn to the soup setting.
11. Cook for 20 minutes.
12. Season with the oregano, thyme, hot sauce, salt and pepper.

Nutritional Information per Serving

Calories 648

Total Fat 29 g

Cholesterol 212 mg

Sodium 511 mg

Potassium 1.7 g

Total Carbs 14.7 g

Protein 25.1 g

Substitution/s:

14 ounces of canned tomato sauce may be used in place of fresh tomatoes. Halibut may be replaced with red snapper or cod.

Fish Biryani

Yields: 4 servings

Serving size: 1 salmon fillet, 1 cup cauliflower rice

Preparation Time: 5 minutes

Cooking Time: 15 minutes

Passive Time: 0 minutes

Total Time: 20 minutes

Ingredients

- 2 tbsp. coconut oil
- ½ yellow onion, chopped
- 15 oz. coconut milk
- ½ tsp. ground nutmeg
- 1 tbsp. garlic powder
- 1 tsp. cardamom
- ½ tsp. ground cloves
- 1 bay leaf
- ½ tsp. ground cinnamon
- 1 tsp. ground cumin
- ½ tsp. ground ginger
- 4 salmon fillets
- Salt to taste
- 4 cups cauliflower rice

Instructions

1. Press the sauté button on your Instant Pot.
2. Pour in the oil.
3. Add the onions.
4. Cook for 5 minutes.
5. Set the pot to manual.
6. Add the rest of the ingredients, except for the cauliflower rice.
7. Cook on high for 10 minutes.
8. Use the quick release method.
9. Serve the fish with the cauliflower rice.

Nutritional Information per Serving

Calories 583

Total Fat 33.6 g

Cholesterol 78 mg
Sodium 166 mg
Potassium 1.3 g
Total Carbs 15.3 g
Protein 19.7 g

CLAM CHOWDER

Yields: 4 servings

Serving size: 1 bowl

Preparation Time: 15 minutes

Cooking Time: 15 minutes

Passive Time: 0 minutes

Total Time: 30 minutes

Ingredients

- 8 oz. bacon, chopped
- 1 qt. chicken bone broth
- 2 lb. cauliflower florets
- 4 cloves garlic, crushed and minced
- 4 cups celeriac root, peeled and diced
- 1 cup onion, diced
- Salt to taste
- 1 tsp. black pepper
- 1 tbsp. dried thyme
- 16 oz. clam juice
- 7 oz. clams, rinsed and chopped

Instructions

1. Press the sauté button on your Instant Pot.
2. Cook the bacon until crisp.
3. Drain on paper towels.
4. Add the broth and the cauliflower florets.
5. Lock lid in place.
6. Set to manual.
7. Cook on high for 3 minutes.
8. Release the pressure manually.
9. Transfer the cauliflower to a blender.
10. Add the garlic.
11. Pulse until smooth and then set aside.
12. Add the rest of the ingredients into the pot.
13. Mix well.
14. Cover the pot.
15. Press the manual button.
16. Cook on high for 5 minutes.

17. Release the pressure manually.

18. Add the cauliflower puree and mix well.

19. Top with the bacon crisps before serving.

Nutritional Information per Serving

Calories 437

Total Fat 29.3 g

Cholesterol 62 mg

Sodium 1.8 g

Potassium 1.2 g

Total Carbs 19 g

Protein 26.8 g

Yields: 4 servings

Serving size: 1 fish fillet, ½ cup sauce

Preparation Time: 10 minutes

Cooking Time: 15 minutes

Passive Time: 0 minutes

Total Time: 25 minutes

Ingredients

- 1 tbsp. coconut oil
- 4 salmon fillets
- 1 onion, chopped
- 4 cloves garlic, minced
- 1 mango, cut into cubes
- 2 tbsp. lime juice
- ¼ cup coconut aminos
- 1 ginger, chopped
- ½ tsp. salt
- ¼ cup cilantro, chopped
- 2 tbsp. apple cider vinegar
- 2 tbsp. honey
- 1 tsp. fish sauce
- ½ cup bone broth
- 1 green onion, sliced

Instructions

1. Set your Instant Pot to sauté mode.
2. Pour the oil into the pot.
3. Brown the salmon fillets on both sides.
4. Remove the fish from the pot. Set aside.
5. Add the onions, garlic and mango cubes.
6. Cook until the mango cubes have turned a little brown.
7. Press the cancel button.
8. Put the salmon back.
9. Add the rest of the ingredients.
10. Cover the pot.
11. Set to manual.
12. Cook on high for 5 minutes.

13. Do a quick pressure release.

Nutritional Information per Serving

Calories 366

Total Fat 31.8 g

Cholesterol 78 mg

Sodium 199 mg

Potassium 908 mg

Total Carbs 25 g

Protein 22.9 g

Substitution/s:

You may also use a white fish fillet such as cod or halibut in place of salmon.

Yields: 2 servings

Serving size: 1 bowl

Preparation Time: 10 minutes

Cooking Time: 38 minutes

Passive Time: 0 minutes

Total Time: 48 minutes

Ingredients

- 2 tbsp. olive oil
- 1 onion, diced
- 4 cloves garlic, minced
- 1 tsp. ginger, grated
- 4 tomatoes, chopped
- 1 Serrano pepper, minced
- 1 tsp. paprika
- 1 tbsp. coriander powder
- 1 tsp. salt
- ½ tsp. black pepper
- ¼ tsp. turmeric powder
- ½ tsp. chili powder
- ½ tsp. cumin powder
- 1 lb. white fish fillet, sliced into small cubes
- 13 ½ oz. canned tomato sauce
- Cilantro, chopped

Instructions

1. Set your Instant Pot to the sauté mode.
2. Add the oil, onions, garlic and ginger.
3. Cook for 3 minutes.
4. Add the peppers and tomatoes.
5. Cook for 5 minutes.
6. Add the fish cubes and brown both sides.
7. Add all the spices and stir frequently.
8. Add the tomato sauce.
9. Mix well.
10. Cover the pot.
11. Press the chili button.

12. Release the pressure naturally.
13. Garnish with cilantro before serving.

Nutritional Information per Serving

Calories 645

Total Fat 32.4 g

Cholesterol 175 mg

Sodium 2.3 g

Potassium 2.3 g

Total Carbs 29.6 g

Protein 24 g

Substitutions:

The chili powder may be substituted with ¼ teaspoon cayenne pepper.

Faux Mashed Potatoes

Yields: 4 servings

Serving size: 1 cup

Preparation Time: 1 minute

Cooking Time: 5 minutes

Passive Time: 0 minutes

Total Time: 6 minutes

Ingredients

- 1 cup water
- 6 cups cauliflower florets
- 1 tbsp. butter
- Salt and pepper to taste
- ¼ tsp. garlic powder
- 1 tbsp. chives, sliced

Instructions

1. Pour the water into the Instant Pot.
2. Put a steamer basket inside the pot.
3. Place the cauliflower on top of the steamer.
4. Cover the pot.
5. Set to manual and cook on high for 5 minutes.
6. Do a quick pressure release.
7. Transfer the cauliflower to a large platter.
8. Season with the butter, salt, pepper, and garlic powder.
9. Mash with a fork, or use an immersion blender to puree.
10. Top with the chives before serving.

Nutritional Information per Serving

Calories 64

Total Fat 26 g

Cholesterol 8 mg

Sodium 66 mg

Potassium 460 mg

Total Carbs 8.1 g

Protein 3.1 g

Yields: 2 servings

Serving size: 4 asparagus spears & ½ cup tofu

Preparation Time: 5 minutes

Cooking Time: 10 minutes

Passive Time: 0 minutes

Total Time: 15 minutes

Ingredients

- 1 block firm tofu, cut into cubes
- ½ tbsp. onion powder
- 1 tbsp. olive oil
- 2 cups vegetable stock
- 8 spears asparagus, trimmed
- 2 large Romaine lettuces leaves

Instructions

1. Coat the tofu cubes with the onion powder.
2. Set your Instant Pot to the sauté setting.
3. Add the olive oil.
4. Add the tofu and cook until golden brown.
5. Transfer the tofu to a strainer.
6. Pour the vegetable stock into the pot.
7. Put the steamer basket inside.
8. Place the asparagus on top of the steamer.
9. Cover the pot.
10. Set to manual.
11. Cook on high for 3 minutes.
12. Use the quick method for releasing the pressure.
13. Place the asparagus and tofu on top of lettuce leaves and serve.

Nutritional Information per Serving

Calories 123

Total Fat 23.5 g

Cholesterol 0 mg

Sodium 58 mg

Potassium 278 mg

Total Carbs 6.8 g

Protein 6.4 g

Substitution/s:

You may use any type of seasoning or spice for your tofu (e.g. garlic powder, chili powder, or salt and pepper).

Yields: 9 servings
Serving size: 1 roll
Preparation Time: 10 minutes
Cooking Time: 15 minutes
Passive Time: 0 minutes
Total Time: 25 minutes

Ingredients

- 2 tbsp. extra virgin olive oil
- ½ cup onion, chopped
- 2 cloves garlic, crushed and minced
- ½ cup shallots, chopped
- 2 lb. tofu, cut into very small cubes
- ½ tsp. dried oregano
- 1 tsp. dried parsley
- 1 tsp. salt
- 1 tsp. pepper
- 16 oz. marinara sauce
- 2 cups cauliflower rice
- 2 cups vegetable stock
- 1 large cabbage, sliced

Instructions

1. Set your Instant Pot to the sauté mode.
2. Pour the olive oil into the pot.
3. Add the onions, garlic and shallots.
4. Cook for 3 minutes.
5. Add the tofu cubes, oregano, parsley, salt and pepper.
6. Cook until the tofu cubes are golden brown.
7. Stir in the marinara sauce.
8. Let simmer for 2 minutes.
9. Add the cauliflower rice. Mix well.
10. Remove the tofu mixture from the pot, and set aside.
11. Add the vegetable stock to the bottom of the pot.
12. Place the steamer basket inside.
13. Place the cabbage leaves on top of the steamer.
14. Close the lid.

15. Set to manual.
16. Cook on high for 3 minutes.
17. Release the pressure quickly.
18. Let the cabbage leaves cool a little.
19. Top each leaf with the tofu mixture and roll.
20. Secure with a toothpick.

Nutritional Information per Serving

Calories 312

Total Fat 25.2 g

Cholesterol 84 mg

Sodium 554 mg

Potassium 385 mg

Total Carbs 12.6 g

Protein 31.1 g

Yields: 2 servings

Serving size: 1 bowl

Preparation Time: 30 minutes

Cooking Time: 41 minutes

Passive Time: 0 minutes

Total Time: 1 hour and 11 minutes

Ingredients

- 1 spaghetti squash
- 1 cup water
- 2 tsp. olive oil
- 1 onion, chopped
- 3 cups marinara sauce

Instructions

1. Slice the spaghetti squash in half, crosswise.
2. Scoop out the seeds.
3. Pour the water into the Instant Pot.
4. Place a steamer basket inside the pot.
5. Put the squash on top of the steamer basket.
6. Seal the pot.
7. Set to manual.
8. Cook on high pressure for 30 minutes.
9. Then, reduce the heat to low and cook for another 6 minutes.
10. Use the quick pressure release method.
11. Remove the squash from the pot.
12. Shred with a fork.
13. Press the sauté function on your Instant Pot.
14. Pour in the olive oil.
15. Sauté the onions for 3 minutes.
16. Add the marinara sauce.
17. Simmer for 2 minutes.
18. Pour the marinara sauce over the spaghetti squash, and serve.

Nutritional Information per Serving

Calories 257

Total Fat 28.6 g

Cholesterol 4 mg

Sodium 806 mg

Potassium 851 mg

Total Carbs 12.3 g

Protein 4.9 g

Substitution/s:

You may replace the marinara sauce with your preferred low-carb pasta sauce.

STEAMED ARTICHOKE

Yields: 2 servings

Serving size: ½ artichoke

Preparation Time: 5 minutes

Cooking Time: 15 minutes

Passive Time: 0 minutes

Total Time: 20 minutes

Ingredients

- 1 whole large artichoke
- 1 lemon wedge
- 1 cup water
- Any low-carb dipping sauce

Instructions

1. Wash the artichokes under running water.
2. Discard any damaged leaves.
3. Trim the stem and the top parts.
4. Rub the top part with the lemon wedge.
5. Pour the water into your Instant Pot.
6. Add a steamer basket inside.
7. Place the artichoke in the steamer.
8. Seal the pot.
9. Select the manual setting.
10. Cook on high for 15 minutes.
11. Release the pressure naturally.
12. Serve with any low-carb dipping sauce.

Nutritional Information per Serving

Calories 30

Total Fat 11 g

Cholesterol 0 mg

Sodium 60 mg

Potassium 237 mg

Total Carbs 6.7 g

Protein 2.1 g

Vegetable Stew

Yields: 8 servings

Serving size: 1 bowl

Preparation Time: 20 minutes

Cooking Time: 40 minutes

Passive Time: 5 minutes

Total Time: 1 hour and 5 minutes

Ingredients

- 4 tbsp. avocado oil
- 1 onion, diced
- 4 stalks celery, diced
- 3 cups celeriac, cubed
- 4 carrots, diced
- 4 cups vegetable stock
- 15 oz. canned diced tomatoes
- 1 tbsp. salt
- 1 tsp. pepper
- 1 tsp. onion powder
- 2 tsp. garlic powder
- 2 tsp. herbes de Provence
- ¾ cup frozen green peas

Instructions

1. Press the sauté function on your Instant Pot.
2. Add the avocado oil.
3. Cook the onions, celery, celeriac and carrots for 10 minutes.
4. Add the vegetable stock, tomatoes, salt, pepper, onion powder, garlic powder, and herbs de Provence.
5. Cover the pot.
6. Press the beef/stew setting.
7. Set the timer to 30 minutes.
8. Release the pressure manually.
9. Add the peas.
10. Let sit for 5 minutes before serving.

Nutritional Information per Serving

Calories 81

Total Fat 25.3 g

Cholesterol 0 mg

Sodium 988 mg

Potassium 510 mg

Total Carbs 15.7 g

Protein 3 g

Substitutions:

You may also use coconut oil or ghee in place of avocado oil.

Yields: 2 servings

Serving size: 1 cup

Preparation Time: 5 minutes

Cooking Time: 11 minutes

Passive Time: 0 minutes

Total Time: 16 minutes

Ingredients

- 1 lb. fresh green beans, trimmed and sliced
- 2 cups water
- 2 tsp. olive oil
- ½ onion, diced
- 1 clove garlic, crushed and minced
- 8 oz. mushrooms, sliced
- 1 tsp. balsamic vinegar
- Salt and pepper to taste

Instructions

1. Put the green beans in the Instant Pot.
2. Add the water.
3. Seal the pot.
4. Set to manual.
5. Cook on high for 2 minutes.
6. Release the pressure quickly.
7. Transfer the green beans to a strainer.
8. Remove the water.
9. Press the sauté function on your pot.
10. Add the olive oil.
11. Sauté the onions and garlic for 3 minutes.
12. Add the mushrooms.
13. Cook for 5 minutes.
14. Return the beans to the pot.
15. Add the vinegar, salt and pepper.
16. Mix well and let cook for 1 more minute.

Nutritional Information per Serving

Calories 149

Total Fat 25.5 g
Cholesterol 12 mg
Sodium 29 mg
Potassium 886 mg
Total Carbs 23 g
Protein 8.1 g

Pinto Bean Dip

Yields: 2 servings

Serving size: 1 cup

Preparation Time: 5 minutes

Cooking Time: 28 minutes

Passive Time: 8 hours

Total Time: 8 hours and 33 minutes

Ingredients

- 3 cups dry pinto beans
- 6 cups water, divided
- 1 onion, quartered
- 3 cloves garlic
- 3 tbsp. red wine vinegar
- 1 tsp. salt
- 1 tsp. ground cumin
- 1 tsp. chili powder

Instructions

1. Place the pinto beans in a large bowl.
2. Add 2 cups of water.
3. Soak for 8 hours.
4. Drain the beans.
5. Add the beans to the Instant Pot.
6. Add 4 cups of water to the pot.
7. Seal the pot.
8. Turn it to the manual setting.
9. Cook on high pressure.
10. Set the timer to 28 minutes.
11. Release the pressure naturally.
12. Place the beans in an immersion blender along with the rest of the ingredients.
13. Puree until smooth.
14. Serve with low-carb crackers.

Nutritional Information per Serving

Calories 262

Total Fat 13 g

Cholesterol 72 mg

Sodium 310 mg

Potassium 1.05 g

Total Carbs 7.3 g

Protein 19.8 g

Substitution/s:

Red wine vinegar may be replaced with lemon juice.

GARLIC BUTTER SPINACH

Yields: 4 servings

Serving size: 1 cup

Preparation Time: 5 minutes

Cooking Time: 20 minutes

Passive Time: 0 minutes

Total Time: 25 minutes

Ingredients

- 1 tbsp. butter
- 1 onion, chopped
- 2 tsp. garlic, minced
- 6 cups spinach
- 1 turnip, chopped
- ½ cup vegetable stock
- Salt to taste

Instructions

1. Put all the ingredients inside your Instant Pot.
2. Seal the pot.
3. Set to manual.
4. Cook on high for 20 minutes.
5. Release the pressure naturally.
6. Serve while warm.

Nutritional Information per Serving

Calories 115

Total Fat 26.2 g

Cholesterol 15 mg

Sodium 233 mg

Potassium 712 mg

Total Carbs 13.3 g

Protein 4 g

Substitution/s:

You may use kale or collard greens instead of spinach.

STEAMED BRUSSELS SPROUTS

Yields: 2 servings

Serving size: 1 cup

Preparation Time: 1 minute

Cooking Time: 3 minutes

Passive Time: 0 minutes

Total Time: 4 minutes

Ingredients

- 1 cup water
- 1 lb. Brussels sprouts
- 1 tbsp. olive oil
- Salt and pepper to taste
- ¼ cup pine nuts

Instructions

1. Place the steamer basket inside the Instant Pot.
2. Add the water.
3. Place the Brussels sprouts on top of the steamer.
4. Seal the pot.
5. Set to manual.
6. Cook on high for 3 minutes.
7. Do a quick pressure release.
8. Drizzle the olive oil all over the Brussels sprouts.
9. Season with the salt and pepper.
10. Top with the pine nuts before serving.

Nutritional Information per Serving

Calories 136

Total Fat 19.7 g

Cholesterol 11 mg

Sodium 29 mg

Potassium 492 mg

Total Carbs 11.4 g

Protein 5 g

Substitution/s:

You may also use walnuts or almonds instead of pine nuts.

CONCLUSION

The low-carb diet is indeed a good first step towards a healthier lifestyle. It will not only help you achieve the weight you've always desired, it will also help keep health problems at bay.

To make the most out of the benefits of this diet, use an Instant Pot, which can help you make delicious and healthy meals without requiring you to spend too much time inside the kitchen. It truly is one of the most convenient cooking devices that you'll ever use.

Happy cooking!

AND PLEASE...

If you'd like more quality diet books at this low price, we'd really appreciate a review on Amazon. The number of reviews a book has is directly related to how it sells, so even leaving a very short review will help make it possible for us to continue to do what we do.

SOURCES

[1] https://www.ncbi.nlm.nih.gov/pmc/articles/PMC4703222/

[2] https://www.ncbi.nlm.nih.gov/pubmed/15468523/

[3] https://www.ncbi.nlm.nih.gov/pmc/articles/PMC3151731/

[4] https://www.webmd.com/diabetes/glucose-diabetes#1

[5] https://www.endocrineweb.com/conditions/type-1-diabetes/what-insulin

[6] https://www.medicalnewstoday.com/articles/180858.php

[7] https://www.healthline.com/health/type-2-diabetes/facts-ketones

[8] https://www.ncbi.nlm.nih.gov/pmc/articles/PMC1325029/

[9] https://www.ncbi.nlm.nih.gov/pubmed/23604708

OTHER BOOKS BY CHEF EFFECT

To find out more about other books that we have written, please visit our Author Central Page by going to the webpage below or scanning the QR code.

https://goo.gl/5IUi6k

Made in the USA
Las Vegas, NV
18 February 2022

44179820R00061